D1783804

Every Woman wants Four Men
Every Man wants Two Women

by
Mr. B

Reviews

In **Every Woman Wants Four Men, Every Man Wants Two Women**, Mr. B shares provocative and valuable insight into how to be an ideal partner. He advises a home free of judgment and labels, allowing couples to openly and fearlessly communicate their true selves and desires in order to create a strong and lasting relationship.

Cheri Torres, Author and Catalyst for Positive Change

B's work helped me to not only improve my sex life, but also to understand the psychology of women on a whole new level. Without his understanding of the needs of women, I'd be lost in my romantic relationships. Thanks B!

Nick Conedera, Filmmaker and Owner of Conedera Studios

Copyright © 2018 by Bertram "Mr. B" Belmontes
All rights reserved. This book or any portion thereof
may not be reproduced or used in any manner
whatsoever without the express written permission of
the publisher except for the use of brief quotations in
a book review.

Printed in the United States of America

First Printing, 2018

ISBN 9781791559403

www.AuthorMrB.com

Contents

TO MY AMAZING WIFE

I could not have completed this without
you by my side being supportive and
being all in, all the way, and what
we have now just blows my mind.

Being a statistic of the rapidly growing rate of divorce in this country and indeed around the world, I was determined to not just settle for the fact that two previous marriages simply just didn't work out.

How could this be? I was raised in a great household with parents who have been, to date, married for 63+ years. So I knew it was possible for a marriage or relationship to last longer than 4 to 5 years, and most importantly be rewarding and fulfilling.

And because I live and breathe everything I've written in this book, I am confident that you too can have that fulfilling type of relationship. At the time of writing this book I have celebrated my 10-year Wedding Anniversary, and am still experiencing the newly wed feeling.

Chapter 1

Introduction

This book is designed to enhance already strong relationships and give a different perspective on what it takes to experience a fulfilling, lasting relationship. It is not designed to manipulate someone, or to take advantage of the opposite sex. It is not a "How to Pick up Chicks" guide. I am also not here to tell you what to do if you are in a struggling relationship. However, there were a few couples who were committed to making things work when it started getting a bit complacent, and after explaining the concept of this book, they were able to reignite the passion, which is proof positive that embracing this methodology works, especially when both parties want the same results.

THIS IS NOT A GAME! However, it is interesting to note that when a guy can effectively talk to a girl, "He got game", or if he cannot seem to get the right words out, he is considered to have "no game". Of course, a woman will tend to be a bit on-guard when it comes to dealing with the opposite sex. This is the reason why some of the examples of the roles mentioned in this book are really important to secure a fulfilling, lasting relationship.

Before we get into the explanation of the "Four Men and the Two Women" statement, we will first address the misconceptions of each title, then get into the explanation as to why these titles apply. We will then give examples, given by real people, who gave their view of what each title means to them, and we will then give additional examples of each category.

We will begin with what The Four Men and The Two Women are.

THE FIRST MAN IS: THE FATHER FIGURE.

THE SECOND MAN IS: THE BEST FRIEND

THE THIRD MAN IS: THE HANDYMAN.

THE FOURTH MAN IS: THE MANDINGO LOVER.

Now for the two women:

THE FIRST WOMAN IS: THE LADY IN THE STREETS.

THE SECOND WOMAN IS: THE FREAK IN THE SHEETS.
(AS IT IS POPULARLY KNOWN IN AN USHER SONG "YEAH").

Now, you already see based on the titles alone why a section of each chapter will be designed to clear up any misconceptions. The titles have a specific purpose which I will clarify, and you will then have a full understanding as to why those titles work best. The accounts in this book are the results of simply listening to people. I have found that people will tell you what they need, want, and desire — if you ask the right questions and listen to the answers. However, when approached as a study, folks will tell you what they think you want to hear. True, there is a small group of people who are not quite sure of what they want, even when asked.

I have never been one who believed that I should "settle" in life, and you should never settle in life either! The ability to not settle begins with you being very clear on everything you deserve in life and what your wants, needs, and desires are. This will require some soul-searching. Take some "alone" time. In those quiet moments, get to know the true you. Always remember: you can choose to be untruthful to anyone, but never to yourself!

I have heard many men say that they have no idea what a woman wants, and some have even read books in an attempt to understand women. If you are one of these men I applaud you, as it means you are willing to cast arrogance aside. There was a time when I shared in that same frustration. There was even a movie made to address that, titled What Women Want starring Mel Gibson. It was a comedy love story, where the guy gets his girl, and the girl gets her man. I am here to tell you that you do not need to get struck by lightning or be electrocuted to get your girl, or for the girl to get her man. What seemed interesting to me was that I noticed the same trends and needs exhibiting itself even in same-sex relationships; each person has a dominating figure that makes them feel fulfilled. In one same-sex relationship, one dominating need that stood out was the "Best friend." A role that in their belief a man was simply not capable of filling. In another same-sex relationship, the dominating role was — you guessed it — The Freak In The Sheets, but deeper than that was the fact of a truly non-judgmental zone. That does not mean that the other figures should be nonexistent, and even in some people the dominating role changes from day to day, and sometimes even moment to moment. Do not get too frustrated with that statement. Rest assured that once you understand and stay in the roles, you can never go wrong. At times, if you are unsure, you can even ask your partner "which role should I take up now?"

Since being in a relationship should not be a guessing game, if you truly care for each other and want your relationship to grow and flourish, you will need to state your needs openly, and don't leave out the "whys".

Before any statement of a need, you should always have a clear understanding of your "why"; it is so powerful, it shows transparency and vulnerability, and that is one of the foundations to bringing you closer together. I am sure by now you are seeing a strong and definite trend occurring and if not, I will tell you: It is strong communication and never assuming. If open and transparent communication is something you struggle with, I would strongly suggest reading some books on the subject.

I have always believed that I would really want the person I choose to spend the rest of my life with to know everything about me upfront, in order for me to know that they totally accept me for who I am. So be true and stay true to who you are. That factor also let me know, when I offer my love, it will be unconditional. As a matter of fact, anyone in my immediate circle knows that the only love I require is unconditional.

Think about this: parents are supposed to love their children unconditionally. If I am to leave the security of that type of household, then you must believe it will be into that same type of environment, even if you came from a household where your parents never seemed to give you that unconditional love. Break the cycle by loving yourself unconditionally, and accept the mistakes and faults as perfect faults, because those are the things which shaped you; and of course, never compare yourself to another person. While it is okay to admire someone for their accomplishments, or even the material things they have, always stay true to yourself.

Have you ever wondered why it is that there is a high rate of marriages emerging from dating sites? Maybe you have not realized that. However, as an event producer, and professional DJ, I have done many weddings where the couple met online. It is not because they lack social skills, it is mostly because of their online profile, where within the structure of it, there are certain questions asked about yourself that get the brain working. As an exercise to get to know the real you, I would strongly suggest that even if you are in a relationship, pick a popular dating site, and both of you go through the questionnaire, in your own space and time, and fill out all of the questions. Do not hit submit when you are finished; instead, write down the answers, then share your answers with each other. This can be a fun way to be open about what you are looking for. Set expectations, and even strike up a conversation. Do not get into an argument if your answers do not seem to be in sync, simply discuss openly why you answered the questions the way you did. If you are single you can do the same, which will help you to always know exactly what you are looking for, most importantly your "Whys" and how those "Whys" make you feel.

There are many churches in which, before they agree to perform a marriage, you must meet with a pastor, priest, or head of the congregation so that they may consult with the couple before agreeing to perform the ceremony. Some religions even separate the couple, have them fill out a questionnaire, then bring them back together to compare answers. If the couple are too far apart on the answers, the officiant many times may refuse to perform the ceremony, suggest certain conversations that a couple needs to have, have the couple attend a retreat of some sort, or attend pre-marriage counseling.

It is very interesting that any one of us who have been to an interview for a job has experienced this. Your potential employer sits down with you and shares all the requirements and expectations of the job you seek. They may ask what you hope to gain by being employed by that establishment, and of course the salary you expect. Now I ask this, if all this needs to happen to get a job, why is it that we jump into relationships without getting in deep about what our wants, desires, needs, and expectations are? Especially if this can be a potentially life long relationship?

Let us keep in mind that everything we have been told and taught still stays true about a good relationship — things like "don't go to bed angry with each other" or "fight fair", "there will be disagreements", "have a date night at least once a week", "always give each other a kiss before you go to sleep and before you leave the house", and the list goes on. All things considered, if those words of advice are followed and practiced, why is it that the rate of divorce has not declined over time instead of increasing? Many couples who follow that adv ce are somehow left wanting more from their mate and their relationship. Due to the upbringing that many have had, people oftentimes tend to stay in the relationship, but somehow are left feeling unfulfilled, just going through the motions, and can end up living an unhappy life. I know that much of this seems a little "doom and gloom", however the facts cannot be disputed: relationships fail, and sometimes for many different reasons. However, if you are a "glass half full" kind of person, then this mean there are 35% of marriages which are successful, and within those marriages, when we focus on the question of what it takes, many of them come back with COMMUNICATION. It is the key. One such couple, my parents. They have been married for sixty-two years. When they speak about what it takes, you listen very carefully.

Our intentions are very honorable in the beginning, and after following sayings and traditions passed down through time, let us keep in mind that times are always changing, and we end up being frustrated wondering if that is what life is all about when it comes to our relationships. Of course things can get boring over time, that is mostly in part because familiarity breeds content, but I do promise you this: if you stay true to being The Four Men and The Two Women all the time, it will take you to heights unimaginable. What level you engage with the roles is something you should have a conversation about together with your partner.

I will say this: no one is looking for you to change who you are. The information in this book is designed to provide the tools it takes to enjoy a fulfilling relationship, and not feel like there is something missing. Many of us are already aware of the roles in this book, and some of us even practice these roles, however it may not be consistent, or even enjoyable to us. There have been many relationships which have failed, where one side of the party said "I have done everything, and still it did not seem like enough" (this from a divorced husband), or "Nothing could make this person happy" (from a separated wife). For the man, after talking with him, and explaining about The Four Men, by himself he was able to identify which one he was not and how he was trying to over compensate in other areas. While he felt that it was enough, clearly it was not, as his wife filed for a divorce. In this particular case, he was not fulfilling the role of The Best Friend. I will get more in depth with his story in The Best Friend chapter.

Now for the separated wife — she did everything she thought would make him happy, however because of her upbringing there were many taboos surrounding sex, and these were not discussed before or at any point during the relationship, so this wife did her best and tried to over compensate in what she thought a good wife was "supposed to do". After talking with her and explaining about The Two Women, she spoke out on her own, and said while she felt she was not The Freak in the Sheets, she honestly believed she could have made her husband happy in other ways, and that their vows should have been enough for

16

him to stick it out. I need everyone reading at this moment to think back to a previous breakup or even divorce and be brutally honest, like the subjects earlier on, and identify which role or roles you were not. Were you consistent enough in those roles? Did you fulfill all of them? Or maybe you were with someone who you realized was not in fulfilling all of their roles.

I have discovered that part of why many relationships tend to get a little stale is because intimacy is very cyclical, and therefore becomes routine. There were many couples that when asked, without hesitation, can tell how many times a week or a month they have sex, what settings are ideal to get them in the "mood", or have admitted that sex is very routine for them, and do not even know why they have not tried to switch things up. One couple admitted that they engage in sex because it helps them sleep well on the nights they were having a tough time falling asleep. One couple used sex just as a stress reliever. There is nothing wrong with those practices, however true passion and intimacy goes bye-bye. Other couples indicated that sex and intimacy only occurred on special occasions: birthdays, anniversaries, holidays, and vacations. Now while I will suggest switching up where you engage in intimacy (Keep it Legal), what I am really referring to is staying in a constant state of intimacy; it is in that state that infidelity and boredom are wiped away. Of course that does not mean you need to be always all over each other, however staying true to your roles is what will place you on that path.

Try to discover other forms of intimacy together, outside of just the physical and yes, there are many other forms of intimacy. Have fun discovering them together.

Chapter 2
The Father Figure

    How can we be a father figure to our lady? Especially when she already has a father. Let us explore the many roles a father plays in her life. A father loves unconditionally, he is supportive, he is the protector, and a provider. In this world there are two types of people: the ones who lead their lives by emotions and the ones who lead their lives by decisions. A person that is emotional leads a roller coaster life, every situation that is emotional effects the direction they take. However, a person who make a decision is able to see that decision all the way through. It is that mindset which is the formula for someone to love unconditionally. In this chapter I will cover many examples of some of the things that the father figure will be, and you can then take these examples and build on them to suit your personal situation. First, I want to eliminate any misconceptions about the title (Father Figure), because the role of a Father Figure as I describe it is totally different than being bossy, controlling or the stereotypical older man. In fact, we many times confuse maturity with age, don't we? While many men might prove the opposite to be true, it is often a result of their surroundings, teachings and upbringing. Let us first keep in mind that you are dealing with someone who is your equal, not beneath you in anyway. I will also give examples given to me by actual couples in situations where the father figure is embraced.

The first example will be the obvious. If in your relationship there are children, your partner will certainly be looking to you to see how you interact with the child or children. Many times they will be looking for the same traits that they observe from the relationship to be transferred to the way you interact with the children. At that time do not hold back the same personality traits from your partner. This is very important that you pay close attention, since many relationships can become distant when all focus is directed to just the child or children. At times resentment and jealousy is close to follow. If you are in a relationship where there are no children involved, that does not mean that you are quite off the hook, because as mentioned earlier on, your partner will still be looking to you to possess those traits.

We will now go through the traits a Father Figure will possess. First of all, as mentioned before, but it is worth mentioning again, a father figure loves unconditionally, meaning they are not going to stop loving you, even if they are upset with you, if you gained weight, if you've lost weight, if you are not feeling well, if you are going through stresses... In other words, your love should never be held back as a ransom. It should be given freely, abundantly and consistently. It is only then, once you have decided to give that level of love, that your partner will feel a high level of security, the same type of security that every child feels when they have a strong nurturing father in their lives. A father figure is also the protector and defender. This is also done without conditions. It is this trait that causes many women to seek out the "bad boy" image in some men. It is that need to feel secure and protected at all cost. However, the "bad boy" image normally comes at a high price and you need to ask yourself, what am I willing to sacrifice for that one trait. Any man is quite capable to be your protector and your defender. He must decide if he is willing to make the ultimate sacrifice for his partner, because he knows that his partner is willing to do the same. Keep in mind that none of this can be easily achieved without open and honest communication, and to achieve that, a person must first and foremost know themselves totally, should be able to communicate clear "Whys" for every decision they make, and should expect the same from their partner — especialy since communication is a two-way street, and a great communicator starts off being a great listener. Practice with each other! It will go a long way.

Next, a father figure is a great leader. This trait has many misconceptions. First, a leader in this sense is not someone who is bossy, demanding or aggressive. In truth and in fact a leader is usually a great follower. Seeking positive role models and examples, he is willing to expand his knowledge by reading and seeking out other positive role models. This can be achieved by simply listening. He is always willing to work together with his partner to achieve future goals.

Ask any woman if she wants to be with a man

who collaborates and supports her goals, in order to also achieve their common goals. I will tell you the answer, they will all stick to a man with these traits.

This is just the beginning of the 4 men.

Anyone who is a parent can relate to what I am about to tell you. I have two daughters, and I want the absolute best for them. I strive for them to be more successful, and better than myself. I want more for them than I want for myself. I genuinely feel the same about my wife, jumping in with both feet to support all of her dreams, and we have conversations on a regular basis about what those dreams are, with no sort of expectations for any reciprocation. The feeling comes naturally when you stay in your roles and stay in that intimate state. Reflecting on my own role as the Father Figure, I have realized that my biggest fans, supporters, and my very own cheering section are my wife and daughters.

Most importantly, a Father Figure is never judgmental! Later in this book, you will see exactly why there is such importance in that trait.

This trait of being judgmental, you may want to stay clear away from! It is like kryptonite to a super relationship, since once judgment is passed, communication and everything else that goes along with a great relationship is dead. I am deliberately using harsh words to reinforce how terrible being judgmental can be. Let us think about this! The moment we step outside our home every day, whether we realize it or not, someone is passing some sort of judgment on us. While driving, someone is making a judgment on the way we drive, the type of car we drive, the color of our car, what the bumper sticker says about us... It is never ending! Of course the worst type of judgment is self judgment. It is only fair that our home should first and foremost be established as a totally judgment-free and label-free zone. Speak it into existence. Have a discussion and come to an agreement that your home should and will become a JUDGMENT-FREE ZONE, and agree to hold each other accountable if either of you observe the other passing judgment. Always remember this poem.

I Wanted to Change the World!

When I was a young man, I wanted to change the world.

I found I could not change the world, so I tried to change my nation.

When I found I could not change the nation, I began to focus

On my town. I could not change the town and as an older man,

I tried to change my family.

Now, as an older man, I realize the only thing I can change is

myself, and suddenly I realize that if long ago I had changed

myself, I could have made an impact on my family.

My Family and I could have made an impact on our town.

This impact could have changed the nation and I could indeed have changed the world.

Author: Unknown Monk 1100 A.D.

Have this discussion and agree to make your home a judgment-free and label-free zone. It will take your relationship to amazing heights.

The following story I have shared with many women, and their responses usually go something like this:

"WOW, I WISH MY MAN DID STUFF LIKE THAT!"

"WHERE CAN I MEET A MAN LIKE THAT?"

"THAT STUFF DOES NOT REALLY HAPPEN."

Gentlemen: this is the perception of some ladies about us.

Here's that amazing story (sarcastically):

It was the weekend, and this couple had two vehicles. Hubby had a two-door coupe, and had to go to the neighborhood hardware store. He asked to use his wife's SUV. When he got into the vehicle he noticed the tank was a little low on fuel, so he decided to fill the tank, pass the SUV through the car wash, vacuum the interior, and came back home and mentioned nothing of what was done. His wife noticed as soon as she got into the SUV on Monday morning. In this scenario the Father Figure is always considerate.

This amazing story has many women just drooling over the gesture. What is even more amazing is the fact that the simplest things can make your lady feel like a queen, it simply requires paying close attention to minor details, and all it took was a little time, so don't be so busy that you have your lady wishing to be around someone else.

Here is another story, which occurred in a group setting of both men and women, (Dirty Minds! Not that type of group!) at a corporate event, where the guest speaker (who also happens to be a great personal friend) was Jon Vroman, founder of The Front Row Foundation, and author of The Front Row Factor. The topic was not just asking questions but asking the **right** question. This question was asked to the group.

WHAT IS THE ONE THING YOU DO THAT MAKES YOUR PARTNER THE HAPPIEST?

An incorrect way to ask that question would be:

IS THERE ANYTHING THAT MAKES YOU HAPPY?

The men started rattling off answers. "Jewelry." one man shouted with confidence. Another chimed in "trips to exotic destinations!" Yet another gave some input "a nice car". The women, not wanting to be left out, started giving their two cents about their men, "great food and cooking" was one woman's contribution. Not wanting to be outdone, this one lady shouted out confidently "Give him some great head" well that one brought the house down with very nervous laughter, and once calmness was restored, all bets were off, and the presenter did not object to that answer, so suddenly it was not

25

a PG type of setting anymore. Another lady chimed in "Give him great sex!" The Men, not wanting to be outdone, gave one last contribution "Having a great home in a nice neighborhood." Jon Vroman now thought it was time to get this gathering back on track, and he commented that he thought some of the same things did it: jewelry and nice vacations. He noticed that his wife did not seem to be consistently happy, so he asked her that very same question:

WHAT IS THE ONE THING I DO THAT MAKES YOU THE HAPPIEST?

Her response was, "I am happiest when I lay my head on your chest in bed and I fall asleep." He could have saved himself so much wondering if he had simply asked not just a question, but the right question. I immediately asked my wife the same question when I returned home:

HONEY, WHAT IS THE ONE THING I DO THAT MAKES YOU THE HAPPIEST?

Her response without hesitation, was the same. I now ask questions like that pretty much all the time.

When you are on point as the Father Figure, there is a great feeling of comfort and security that your partner should feel all the time, even when you are not at home. This role should never feel like a chore, as there is no greater feeling than knowing that my partner turns to me for advice and follows it when given. If I do not have the answer we find it together, and because of that, no one is left behind, and we grow and learn together as a couple.

26

"If You're Not Growing Together,

You WILL Grow Apart"

Mr. B

Chapter 3
The Best Friend

While we may all have our own views as to what a Best Friend is, and some of us may have never even had a Best Friend, we must keep in mind what a Best Friend is to our lady. Through the eyes of our lady, there are many instances where a woman, after meeting a man, will introduce him to her closest friend, even before she introduces him to her parents, and may even go by the approval or disapproval from that friend. Women tend to look for advice from a friend and may sometimes share very intimate details in the process. If your lady has a best friend, believe that her best friend knows how you perform, especially if you rocked her world. There is almost no way she will keep that to herself, she will be anxious the morning after for someone to make the comment of how much she is glowing. A woman's best friend will share shopping time, going to shows and concerts. By not doing these things, memories and highlight moments with your lady will be created with someone else. Maybe you are thinking that it may not be a big deal, but I can assure you it is a very big deal, and you are missing out. If your lady tells you that she does not require you to be her best friend, it is simply because you never established yourself as one, however you can create a process to the path of becoming your lady's Best Friend. Later in another chapter I will share an important story shared in a very open interview, which will give you some insight into what is really going on in the minds of some women out there. So now let us look at some of the qualities of a best friend. You will find many of these qualities with the same similarities of the other 3 men described in this book.

A Best Friend, just as the Father Figure, loves unconditionally. They listen to problems shared without labels or judgment. The Best Friend is there through thick and thin, will stand by your side and fight any battle with you. Best Friends do not hold grudges, and although you will fight with your best friend or may not agree on everything, because you respect each other, you can pick up where you left off as though nothing was wrong. A Best Friend is also very genuine, and they will have the difficult conversations with you. Being able to accept your lady as they are is an important part of being a Best Friend. It is not just by being there for her but leading by example and sharing things with her as you would with your own Best Friend because if she senses that things are only one way, then the friendship will end and you no longer have the opportunity to be her Best Friend. This then creates an opening for someone else, male or female, to fill that void.

The following pages contain accounts of both types of scenarios: where a man was his woman's best friend, and where he chose to be disconnected. We're also going to touch on some stories where you can see the importance of the Best Friend in same-sex relationship settings. You can choose which one you would want to be, and you may also notice that routines are like a cancer to a relationship. But remember that sometimes even the strongest of love is not enough to reignite the fire.

In the couple we discuss first, the man worked at a blue collar type of job which was very physically demanding, and all he looked forward to was to get home, take his shoes off, put his feet up, open up a beer and relax. When his lady, who worked in a corporate office, would come home, they would share a kiss, she would go to the kitchen to prepare a meal for them. Since they had no kids, they did agree when they got together that they would always make time for each other. In the beginning, only she established what her needs and wants were, and he simply agreed. However, now there is this real life situation, that in time the intimacy started to fade away. In his mind he felt that as hard as he works in this labor-intensive job that she should understand that he needs to relax, and while she appreciates her hard working man, she would love to have some time with her man, and sometimes when she wanted to talk about her day he would tend to blow her off. Now when they first started living together, whenever she got home, after they shared a kiss they would ask each other how their day went, but with their newfound routines after living together for some time, talking about their day felt like she was nagging or just always complaining. When the weekend came around, he would go socialize with his friends, since he was annoyed with her constant complaining, she would go to the salon to get her nails done, and would get an opportunity to talk about her week with her nail technician. If it was not her weekend at the salon, she would go to visit her mom and they would first start off talking about her job, but then the conversation would go to how frustrated she was with her man, and how ignored she felt. Her mom suggested that she should go lingerie shopping with her man (yes, a pretty progressive mom), and maybe he will notice her to be the sexy woman he got together with in the first place. When she brought up the idea of them spending time together at the store shopping, he got annoyed and said he would stay home since there was lots to do around their home. She is determined to surprise him with her purchases, so she recruits a girlfriend and off to the lingerie store they go. They have a great day talking about all sorts of things, they laugh together, have lunch at the food court at the mall, and she is now excited to show off her purchases back at home.

Later that night they adjourn to the bedroom, he showered before her, and is now in bed waiting for his lady to emerge. She is going the whole nine: makeup, hair, even the high heels. As she emerges from the bathroom he is clearly excited, but makes no mention of the sexy attire she's wearing, so she brings it up, and asks "what do you think of the outfit I wore for you?" To which he replies " I don't know why you spend money on those outfits, since they come off anyway".

Now I ask you, is that in any way a man deserving? No one is telling you that you have to always do what your lady wants you to, or always be out shopping, however if you make some effort, it will go a long way. Of course let her vent from time to time, and if the love you have is unconditional, you will want to spend all that time with your Best Friend. Just keep in mind that if the both of you talk only with your friends, your friends will be all you may end up with, so start the communication process with each other as soon as you can.

The next couple's story takes a totally opposite turn. These two knew of each other from high school. They were not necessarily high school sweethearts, but he was always attracted to her, and always thought to himself that she would never go for a guy like himself. Now, you are maybe thinking 'here's a guy with low self-esteem', and you may be correct, but it worked out in his favor in the long run. We are now several years later, and our guy got his girl. He decided he would treat his wife like a queen, and even though they each had their own car, outside of commuting to and from work, everything else they did together in one vehicle.

It may not seem like a very big deal to be always riding together, however while in the car they talked about everything: current topics, their dreams, their fears, and as the weeks went by, they started sharing their fantasies with each other, and without even realizing it they were becoming Best Friends. Being around each other seemed like the only place that there were no judgments. The man in this relationship had male friends, co-workers, and colleagues, and interestingly whenever he would share his weekend with his wife (which would include shopping for lingerie occasionally), he would be ridiculed, but he always had a clear vision of who his queen was, and since these folks

33

with opinions weren't taking care of his every need he would brush it off, and share less whenever he was around these people.

The Lady in this relationship would do the same with her co-workers and friends, the difference however was that instead of getting ridiculed, everyone was anxious to meet this great guy that goes shopping and helps pick out some sexy outfits.

But ladies, be careful, because some very unscrupulous ladies are paying closer attention than you think, and may begin to want to meet your man in person more enthusiastically than you may want them to. Outside of your relationship, leave some details off the table, don't share everything every time. I leave you with this quote from my Grandfather.

"Eat All, Drink All,

But Don't Talk All"!

— Victor Irving Gabriel

Let's next look at an interview with a same-sex female couple, and how it pertains to being a Best Friend. First, to provide you with a visual description, this is a bi-racial couple, the African American we will call "D" and the Caucasian we will call "L".

D and L started off being best friends for three years. They met online and quickly realized that even though they were opposites, they clicked. Thus began a level of communication that left nothing off the table, and love grew unsuspecting to both D and L, even though they were both in a relationship with men at the time. In an effort to spice things up in their relationship, L invited D to join L and her man in a threesome, and that was all it took. L soon came to the realization that she preferred being with D over her boyfriend of five years, while D also decided to end her relationship with her boyfriend at the same time. She said her main motivator was that with a female there is a greater ability to be totally honest and completely vulnerable with each other, and it seems to be easier with a woman than with a man because men tend to have that guard up to protect their ego.

L then chimed in saying that with a female there's a more emotional connection than physical, and while this is not to say that the physical connection is not great, the emotional connection is something that was lacking in L's relationship. Things even got to a point where she was so deeply craving that connection, but felt like she was always being judged, and became closed off to express herself in anyway — whereas after only two months in a relationship with D, she realized that it was a totally judgment free zone, and a deep love was born between the two.

Divorce or separation of a married couple is certainly not a pleasant thing for anyone to experience, and here is the story of a couple that by the time they discovered what the real issue was, there was already a significant disconnect and it was unfortunately way too late to save the marriage. We'll look at the dynamics of this couple, and maybe you can recognize all that was happening, even though they were not fully aware of what going on.

To begin with, there was a considerable age difference of seventeen years, the wife being the younger of the two. This couple lived together for many years, and in the beginning their communication was great — there was no topic that was off the table. They did everything together, and even though they had their own spaces, for the most part where ever you saw one the other was not too far away. If there were fantasies brought up by either one, they would explore it together and grow stronger together. Even though they lived together, they waited several years before they decided to get married. Having experienced all their hearts desired, even experimenting with threesomes, they both decided it was time to have their first child. For most couples having a child changes a whole lot of how they function together, but not with these two. The timing must have been perfect because they grew even closer, and were able to offer their child so much more; because of their communication style, they were properly prepared to address any conversation with their young child.

Now, let us jump forward seven years, when they get a visit from the husband's childhood best friend and his wife, with their five year old child.

The men decided to go out and catch up on old times. There is lots of laughter and the drinks are flowing... Oh how time flies when you are having a good time! Last call is announced at the bar and these two best friends decide it was time to go back home to their wifes and children, with one last stop to the restroom before their forty five minute drive. They take off, but twenty five minutes into the drive tragedy strikes when they crash into the back of a truck and the visiting best friend dies at the scene. Instantly a wife has lost her husband, and a child is left to grow up without a father.

Even though there are serious consequences to follow from this accident, the husband just shuts down and shut out his wife. Because of his guilt, he spends even more time cherishing his son, thinking of what it would have been like if his own son had to grow up without a father. His wife, seeing the change in her husband, while appreciating the strong bond between father and son, is realizing that she is losing her Best Friend. They don't seem to talk much anymore, and he seems distant and shut off; even during intimate moments there was a disconnect. Determined to stick it out with her husband, the wife suggests they go to counseling, hoping that he would come to terms with his guilt, knowing that a very long time (over seventeen years!) had passed and being concerned about his well-being. Because of his upbringing, he refused to go to any counseling, denying that there was anything wrong with himself or with them, and they could just work things out themselves.

Now that he was aware that his wife was not too happy, he tried to over compensate, serving his wife breakfast in bed, cleaning, catering to all her needs (except talking about what continues to eat him up inside), and they even have another child. In his mind, he is being a good husband to his wife. However, in his wife's mind she has lost her Best Friend, and now life at home seems very routine. Her husband no longer want to go out socially because he feels that if there is any drinking involved he could end up in the same situation which happened seventeen years ago. Not wanting to be unfair to his wife he tells her she can go out to social events with her girlfriends and co-workers, and soon these girlfriends become best friends. Just like best friends do, they talk about any and everything, and since we tend to trust our best friends to always have our best interest at heart, a decision was made that the life she was living with her husband was not making her happy.

Divorce papers were filed stating irreconcilable differences and now she is focusing on her own happiness and seems more at peace, because so much of her life since the accident revolved around supporting her husband emotionally and trying to get back her Best Friend. Finally she chose to give up the fight and concentrate on herself.

"If you don't stand for something, you will fall for anything."

—Malcolm X

Chapter 4
The Handyman

Now judging from the title of this chapter, I'm sure many of you are thinking you may need to take up some classes on how to become a general contractor. Well rest easy because in this context The Handyman does not need to have any repair skills whatsoever, although it certainly will not hurt if you are comfortable with some sort of DIY skills. In this context The Handyman is simply the man who takes care of any and all issues. He steps up to the plate when challenges present themselves. This can also be compared somewhat to The Father Figure, especially if there are any kids involved, being a problem solver to their issues are viewed by your mate in a very positive way, which makes you look like a Knight in shining armor. As we go through this chapter I will give you different examples of what your lady looks for from her Handyman. Make no mistake this figure is a big one since many women have stepped into the path of infidelity because her man stayed away from his duties of being the "I'll take care of it" type of man. No man intends to be shirking their Handyman duties to their lady, it is just a matter of not being informed that his lady is looking for that on a daily basis. We tend to get caught up being a provider, and depending on the way we were raised and environment we have been around, we tend to sometimes think that giving or buying whatever our lady wants will keep her happy, and of course it will, but it is very temporary. I can assure you that if you stick to these Four Men it will not even matter how much you make. Of course a great payday wouldn't hurt, but in reality it's just not a focal point in most cases.

Here is the story of an actual couple where the man in the relationship consistently negated his duties as The Handyman and almost lost his lady to someone else. The first thing happened when his lady mentioned that the brakes in her car were making an awful noise. Instead of driving the car himself to hear the noise, he told her to just take it to the neighborhood auto shop. He was simply dismissive because he had a tough day at work and all he wanted to do was relax in front of the TV. This couple was very well off and money was not an issue, and he felt that because he earned a lot of the money and provided a lavish lifestyle for his lady, it should be enough... But in fact, his lady wanted a different response from her man. So off to the neighborhood auto repair shop she goes.

There was no appointment necessary; she drove into the auto center, went to the counter and was greeted by a very pleasant young man. With a smile, he said "Good evening ma'am, how may we help you today?" To which she replied "my car is making an awful noise when I step on the brakes." He takes down some information from her, such as name, address, and phone number. The young man asked her to ride in the car with him so that he can hear the noises she was describing. As they ride in the car together, she is visibly very upset because she does not know if she can continue to trust having this car. In a very calming voice the young man tells her, "Don't you worry ma'am we will take care of everything." The magic words she would have loved to hear from her husband, however she was now hearing this from this handsome young mechanic.

Upon arriving back to the auto center, the young man leads her to the customer waiting area and asked her if she needed a ride to her home or to her place of work. She decided to wait in the customer service area. He offers her either bottled water or coffee, there is a television in the waiting area, and he offers her the remote and tells her she can change the channel to whatever she would like to watch.

Now so far in this story, how many opportunities are you observing? The young man then tells her one more time, "not to worry ma'am, we will handle everything for you." It is at this point she does not quite see her man as her savior, but because there is still a comfortable lifestyle she overlooks her man's lack of stepping up. However when her car was completed, the pleasant young mechanic calls her up to the counter and tells her the other magic words, "Everything is taken care of, you're all set." She pays her bill and leaves the shop with a smile on her face she remembers everything about this young man and how the repeated words in her head, "I'll take care of it". The same words she longed to hear from her husband.

A couple of weeks later, the dishwasher started leaking onto the kitchen floor. Frustrated, she calls out to her husband, who almost sounded annoyed as he responds to her, "What is the matter?" She explains that there is water all over the kitchen floor and he responded, "What do you want me to do about that?" However, the husband came to investigate what was happening. Disgusted he walks away telling her to place a call to the local appliance repair store. The husband goes back to the other room to resume his normal evening routines. He is confident in the fact that the money that he earns is more than enough to cover any repairs needed.

The following day, the wife goes to the local appliance repair store and this time she is greeted by an older gentleman about the same age as her husband. With a smile he asked her, "How may we help you today?" She goes on to explain her frustrations with the leaking dishwasher, to which he replies, with empathy, "I'm sorry that you had to go through such a tough evening, ma'am." And here it comes... "It will be taken care of."

Now, this scenario is totally different because this repair man is now entering their home to look at the dishwasher, and in the house is just the two of them, with comforting and reassuring words that "This is not a major problem. This happens all the time, just give me a few minutes and it will be all fixed."

Upon repairing the leaky dishwasher and leaving the house, he hands her a business card and tells her of all the different types of household appliances that his company services, and that if she has any more issues not to hesitate to call him directly.

Now my question to you is, "If you were this woman and you now know of two separate, very pleasant men that can take care of your needs, would you continue to ask your man about any other problems?"

It is no secret that women not only fantasize about a man in uniform, but also have many fantasies about the repairman. Back in the day as a cable technician, I never quite understood why I experienced lots of flirting and propositions, a few times even from couples (I found out later they were swingers). As far as they were concerned they had a sea of mostly willing men to choose from, so they would place a trouble call and if attracted to the cable guy, they would make their move, and yes some of these women were married.

One Sunday morning out on a cable repair call, I got to the front door to introduce that I was on location for the service call. This gorgeous lady opens the door fully, not partially hiding behind the door, wearing just a robe opened up at the front and totally nude under the robe. She invited me in, to which I said "I'm sorry, but I would need for you to please make yourself a little more presentable before I can enter into the home." I am of course all man, so while I at least took in the full view that was offered at that front door at that Sunday Morning 8:00am to 10:00am time slot, I was certain that was not the first time this beautiful lady had done this. The point being that many women, whether in a relationship or not, have had fantasies about some sort of handyman.

Another group that can have a whole lot of stories to tell are auto mechanics, and many acquaintances of mine who are in that field have shared their experiences of being approached by many women. Some auto technicians have even met their current wife while in the field.

What is so interesting is a woman's strong sexual attraction to a man that is an "I will take care of it" type of man, but when these women were asked, they could not give a reason why they found this type of man so appealing — but fellas rest assured that you do not need to have any repair skills, just get her issues taken care of and be sure to have your lady see and experience the "after it is fixed" state.

Maybe during a love making session you can tap into what type of handyman drives your woman wild! Afterwards, discuss the "whys", and maybe next time you can recreate that fantasy with you dressed up as that handyman. Feel free to be creative.

Chapter 5

The Mandingo Lover

Many of us have heard the word "Mandingo" used in the porn industry. Mandingo is a porn star with a massive member. First off, the title of this chapter has nothing to do with the size of a man's penis. Let us take a moment to bury the myths about penis size. When is enough, enough? I know what many of you men are thinking: this pep talk is all well and good for most guys, but I have a special problem. Your special problem is the most common source of sexual anxiety among men:

(THE FEAR THAT YOUR PENIS IS TOO SMALL)

The number of men who share this feeling of inadequacy is all out of proportion to the number of men who have small penises, which shows how seriously most men take the supposed value of a large penis. But even the man with the small penis is unfounded in his fears. However glamorous or "manly" it may seem to be "well hung" is not really a factor in intercourse. The size of a man's penis is not a central concern to a woman, who knows from experience that she is equally satisfied by any size, once the man wielding it knows exactly what he is doing.

Here are a couple of facts to consider.

1. The difference in men's penis size is not so pronounced during erection. In other words, men whose penises are large in the flaccid state do not gain as much in size when they attain an erection; and a small penis grows proportionally larger. And let's face it... Do you really care what it looks like in the shower at the gym, or the golf club locker room?

2. Whatever the size, the penis is not the primary instrument for arousing and satisfying a woman. The reality is that penises don't have joints, they have no protruding surfaces, they are relatively inflexible when erect, and it takes a great deal of effort just to make them move even a little bit. You just cannot do much with a penis except wave it around, bat it against something, or move it in and out. The real sexual organs are the hands and the mouth. Whatever the size of your penis, it is worthy of its limited function, and it is fully capable of giving you pleasure as well.

Once you realize that you are NOT defective physically, you will have shot down one of your excuses for not being a good sex partner. But this deprivation will be well worth it, because you will have rid yourself of those self-defeating feelings of inadequacy which deprive many men of sexual fulfillment, and you will be well on your way to becoming that Mandingo lover that your lady deserves.

46

Now that we've established that Mandingo does not describe having a large penis (in fact, it could not be further from the truth), we can start to talk about how this title is used to describe the size of the **lover** that needs to be in every man. When you hear the word Mandingo, you automatically think massive, which will become clear in some of the stories we will look at in this chapter. Interestingly enough, men who are well endowed will not be reading a book like this, and therefore will almost certainly lack being the **massive lover** that every woman deserves and desires, because accounts from many women who have experienced men like this all return with a common result: well-endowed men are often very arrogant about their size and turn out to be very selfish, insensitive lovers. In this chapter we will take you as far away as possible from that type of thinking.

Every Mandingo Lover must first follow a certain code of ethics.

1. He is always upfront and honest about his intentions.

Keep in mind that this is not a license for sexual harassment, which leads to the next point...

2. He has total respect for his lady.

Never say the words "I Love You" to get into a woman's pants, as that will always backfire on you. (Plus, you know what they say about Karma?) However, when those words are spoken, it is because he is willing to go for the long haul and offer that love unconditionally. He always views his lady as his equal, never inferior or beneath him. He NEVER, and I repeat NEVER, raises his hands to her under no circumstances. If you ever have that much anger towards your lady that you somehow feel compelled to raise your hands at her, simply leave her, because she deserves someone better. That statement I make absolutely no apologies for, and now that it is in writing, go ahead and hold me to it. Just as bad as physical abuse is mental abuse; words can cut like a knife, so if you can't tell and show her that she's beautiful and sexy every chance you can, then don't be selfish and keep her from finding true happiness, because I can assure you if she's not feeling like the most beautiful woman in the world around you, then she's not truly happy, and a domino effect tends to follow.

One Man's Trash Is Another Man's Treasure

In this context the Mandingo lover educates himself and expands his knowledge on pleasing his partner. He is willing to ask questions and is open to directions from his partner on what it takes to deliver Mandingo-style loving. The term Mandingo also does not mean porn-type sex of any kind. Keeping in mind the type of sex in porn is a purely fictitious accounts of what true intimate experiences should be, I'd like to clarify that I am in no way trying to steer you away from watching or liking porn, or that having fetishes is a bad thing. Remember: I am not here to judge. Please always be upfront about your desires and fetishes to your partner or potential partner. As I've said many times already, open communication is key to the path of becoming a true Mandingo lover. I would love to know that the woman that I choose to be intimate with matches me in every way because she has accepted the true me sexually, and I am certain you would want the same. There is someone for

48

everyone out there, and when you get to know yourself, and what you want and desire, and most importantly the "whys", you will be much more likely draw the right match to yourself. (Here we are in Chapter Five, and I'm sure by now you've noticed the recurring theme of the "whys". Be prepared to see it pop up quite a few more times!)

I have a question for you: do you know how many erogenous zones there are on the female body?

The Female Body is Truly a Beautiful Thing!

While every woman's body is unique, there are a few areas that tend to make many women quiver with pleasure. As you stimulate these sensitive erogenous zones, you will leave your lady's skin tingling with pure bliss. Pick a new zone to play with each love-making session, or set time aside on a Saturday morning as you lay in bed just being lazy (turn that television off, unless you're watching something sexy and erotic), and explore all of her hot spots in succession. By the time your turn comes around, she will be anxiously aching to reciprocate for those mind-blowing full body orgasms.

We will have some tips for her about you in the "Freak in The Sheets" Chapter.

A non-Mandingo lover just knows kissing, breast play, maybe oral sex, the clitoris, and of course penetration. While he will be able to achieve his woman experiencing an orgasm, what's sad is that many women have been trained to settle for that level of satisfaction. Some women have been known to adjust their bodies to match their

49

lover's moves to achieve the maximum pleasure, but somehow they are left with a feeling of wanting "more", without ever fully understanding what that "more" is. A Mandingo Lover, however, has the ability to provide a very fulfilling experience which will keep on delivering even after the act. For instance, he understands there are many different types of orgasms that a woman is able experience, each one having a different feel, sensation and body experience (and he is OK with the fact that she may not be open to try all types). The most common and widely known is the clitoral orgasm, next is the G-Spot orgasm, and another is from penetration (which, depending on the penis shape, can stimulate both the clitoris and the G-Spot at the same time), and finally anal orgasms. The second and fourth have been known to produce squirting orgasms, and yes, achieving intense orgasms ultimately should be a goal of yours.

Every woman has many erogenous zones, and you will need to explore them together with your woman, keeping in mind that they can vary greatly from woman to woman! A great way to locate them and open her up to the experience that keeps on delivering is through massage. You can use a search engine to identify some zones, and have her tell you what it feels like. While the beginning of this exploration may quickly lead to more, be sure to exercise some restraint at this point. I promise you, it will pay-off later on.

Exploring Around Her Body

The Collarbone

This often-overlooked area is a field of erotic energy. Work your way outward from the collarbone and stimulate the sensitive skin under her arms.

The Sides Of The Breast

News Flash! The nipple is not the breast! While the non-Mandingo lover will tend to focus on this one area, the fact is that other parts of the breast are craving your sensual touch. Many women have reported that the sides of the breast (close to the under arm) and the area above the areola are actually the most erotic zones for kissing, licking, and sucking. This is the reason why many women have no problem with a little breast self-examination while in the shower, but would much prefer to have you — her lover — performing that task. Keep in mind that this pair of beautiful mounds are not actually identical — each breast differs in appearance (unless enhanced) and sexual response, so find out from her if she favors one over the other.

Some women have experienced some massive orgasms from breast play, so be sure to follow any guidance she may offer.

The Back of the Knees

Make her "weak in the knees" right away by breathing gentle kisses against the skin of this very common, but often overlooked, sweet spot.

The Inner Thighs

Maybe it's the inner thigh's proximity to her love-tunnel, or perhaps it is the rich, sensitive nerve endings and veins that cross paths with her vagina... Whatever the reason, this sweet real estate of skin is often highly responsive to a gentle touch, kisses, or even licks.

The Small Of her Back

As mentioned earlier in the section on breasts, some women can reach an orgasm through breast stimulation only, but did you know that some women can become aroused and even have an orgasm from having the small of their back rubbed or licked?

The Brain

A great misconception is that men think about sex more than women during the day, and our ladies are quite content letting us believe that to be true. The truth is that accounts given by many women show that they think about intimacy more than us men, they are just better at keeping those thoughts at bay, or not acting out on it. In fact many have even found themselves masturbating and having orgasms while in the workplace, or even driving in traffic! Sorry ladies, secret revealed! If this is you, please share with your man... If you think he can handle it! (I say that because the reason many women don't share things like that with their men is because of the reputation that men have fragile egos. Well, ladies, a real Mandingo Lover's ego is never fragile, so do share and see the amazing heights it will take your relationship.)

Given this new information of how easy it is for some women to either satisfy themselves or even have orgasms, you would then understand why you would need to step your game up, and become the Mandingo Lover that you know your woman deserves. I will let you in on this little secret, which I'm sure that many of you may already know (if you did not know just pretend and say you did): the most responsive sexual organ in a woman is her brain!

Fantasizing about an erotic hookup activates the area of the brain associated with orgasms and sends arousing oxytocin throughout your system. This is why experts call the mind a human's largest sex organ, why some women can think themselves off, and why 37 percent can reach their peak even while they're sleeping! Therefore, if you can tap into your lady's fantasies with a bit of sexy talk, it can be way hotter than anything you can do with your hands or lips. If you tend to have some trouble getting started with the dirty talk, just begin with sexy compliments about her body or her skills as a lover. Start slowly and take some time to talk about your feelings and reactions to the things you both said in the heat of the moment after the hot steamy sex is over. This certainly is the path to taking your relationship and intimacy to the next level.

For this reason, a woman is, and should be, very protective of her brain, and should be very wary of who she lets into her head. This is the reason why, in the beginning of the book, I explained that this book is not about manipulation of any sort, but a clear understanding that a woman must have ultimate trust in you before she let you into her head. This is a big part of the reason many women expect their men to be a one-woman kind of man. It is, on the other hand, why some women make the decision to stay single and date multiple men, because guys just don't seem to step up to the plate. However, when a woman lets you into her head, be sure to let her guide you to what type of communication she finds stimulating, however do not become too dependent on her guidance. Your goal after the initial guiding is to take control, and build on what you have been instructed. You can do this by taking the time to educate yourself with books. Two of my go-to titles, "The Sensuous Man" and "The Sensuous Woman", are unfortunately no longer in print, however there are many places on the Internet you can pick up a second-hand copy. If you're unable to locate them, try to occasionally read some of the articles in the women's magazines, like Vogue and Cosmopolitan. In those magazines, many women are willing to tell you exactly what they want, you just have to be willing to listen and understand where they are coming from. It may seem silly, but I must insist that you take this very important step ladies and gentlemen! (I say ladies also because this also applies to same-sex relationships, however because many women in same-sex relationships tend not to rush through their intimate sessions, they usually do not lack in this area. Sorry fellas.)

Here are some highlights from an interview with a bi-racial same-sex female couple. They both self-identify as bi-sexual, because they occasionally have sex with men, but described the sex between themselves as mind-blowing. What follows should be eye opening.

"L" has the highest sex drive of the two, and also tends to be submissive. She had a four year relationship with a guy, but ended it after meeting "D". She felt that every time she expressed her desire to experiment, her boyfriend would come across as very judgmental, and with "D" having a dominant personality, these two were a perfect match. There are no discussions between these two that is taboo, there is zero jealousy between them, and they made a pact that there will never be any judgments or labels. Remember in the Father Figure chapter where I said that judgments are like kryptonite to a relationship? Well here it is straight from a female that put up with it for four years and had enough.

The Cherry Halls Technique

There are many books out there that offer all sorts of sexual tips and tricks geared toward both genders, but after sharing this with many couples, the feedback was extremely positive, and it was requested by many. I thought I should share that tip with you.

Go out and pick up a pack of cherry-flavored Halls. It must be the cherry flavor, as any other flavor may tend to be too strong. Start with it beginning to dissolve in your mouth as you work your way down to her love tunnel. By the time you have reached your destination you will be offering the perfect sensation. Be aware this will lead to one of the quickest climaxes she will ever experience!

As a couple, you can each suck on one, or

share it in a kiss and maybe get into a 69 position. Warning: the sensations are highly addictive, and the orgasms are extremely explosive.

Chapter 6
The Lady in the Streets

To start off this chapter, I'd like to clarify that for the purpose of this book, The Lady in the Streets is the woman who knows all the ethics that go along with being a true lady. First and foremost, cleanliness is next to godliness. A Lady in the Streets makes sure she is always fresh and clean. She knows that she is never to mess around with a married man, or any other woman's man for that matter, which I know can be a tough one for some women to follow.

This book, as well as that fact, are not about judgment, however know that there are serious repercussions that never end well, so remember this chapter when things comes to that point. The Lady in the Streets knows to love her man unconditionally and reminds him of that fact constantly, as she is the main reason he noticed her in the first place (that and her body of course... Remember we are very visual creatures). She also maintains balance within the household and never holds back intimacy as a form of reward. She sticks by her man through thick and thin. A Lady in the

Streets is generally what some men call "marrying material". That is not to say that if getting married is not your thing, that you are not to be a Lady in the Streets. These are simply the qualities that every man seeks. Here are some scenarios of real couples where it was fully understood what a Lady in the Streets entails.

The first is a couple where the husband is a very successful businessman. There was a corporate function and spouses were invited to attend. His wife was introduced around and was quite popular. You could even say she was a hit. That was mainly because she knew about current events. She was able to hold intelligent conversations. She knew no one wins when talking about politics, and even when backed into a corner with a political conversation, she would very smoothly change the subject. Of course, the folks that tried to hear her opinions realized how smoothly she was able to change the subject, and in turn really respected her for this. The result was that every following event for years to come, even if spouses were not invited, she was invited by his colleagues by name. All of this is to say that she left an obvious, lasting impression.

Simply put, while the Lady in the Streets demands respect, she can just as easily earn it. She is her man's most loyal best friend, and never judges him. She knows when to lead, in the sense that she can quickly earn her man's trust in her as a best friend, and the type of communication she requires from her best friend is the same type of communication she offers to her man. For instance, if you want your man to tell you his deepest fantasies you must be the first to lead by sharing your own fantasies. If you want your man

58

to tell you his fears, you are going to have to lead by sharing your fears. There is an old saying that a relationship is a 50/50 situation. However I feel that implies that some sort of score is kept. I am here to tell you a strong relationship that lasts through all struggles is in fact a 100/100 type of relationship, meaning that both sides are all in 100% with no tabs being kept. Once you go down that path of keeping tabs, everything is truly doomed.

The Lady in the Streets also follows a very strict code of ethics, some of which have been passed down through many generations. Sometimes this even includes the conversations that a mother of a bride-to-be would talk about. While some of these ethics vary between different cultures and demographics, here are just a few to put you on the right path of what a true Lady in the Streets is.

Simply put, when you are with your man, other men tend to crave and wish they had a woman like you. A Lady in the Streets possesses a true sense of power over her man and any man she comes in contact with. Knowing that power, she handles it with humility and grace. It is believed that the only way to truly serve others is to serve yourself first. In order to do that you must truly know yourself fully; while your height, weight, body type, or the color of your eyes describes your appearance, or things you like to eat, things you like to do, or places you like to visit describes your hobbies, many women are not totally sure of who they are. Here is a very important question I would like for you to consider: What is your actual presence when you enter a room, and what presence would you like to have as you enter a room? For the first part of the question, you can consider asking others what is their impression when they first see you. It can be a great conversation piece at gatherings. Keep those two questions in mind because they will make more sense after I tell you this next story.

My youngest of two daughters was going through a few (quite normal) challenges in school. For any of you parents reading this book I'm sure you can relate; some kids just have a harder time fitting in more than others. With my many years as a DJ doing kids parties, mitzvahs and other similar events, I have noticed that many young folks in their pre-teen and teenage years have a tough time with their identity. One day, during my normal Saturday morning conversations with her, mostly following up on the previous week in school, while trying to make certain the topic does not get into school dramas and gossip, I asked her this simple question: "Who are you?"

A look of confusion appeared on her face, which I was not surprised about one bit, and after some bit of thinking, she started to reply with some sort of confidence, "well, Dad, I am about 4' 10", curly hair..." until I stopped her.

"No honey, that is a description of you, who are you?"

The look of confusion turning into frustration, she replied, "I love to draw, I love to play with my games, I like to visit grandma and grandpa..."

Once again I interrupted her, and said "no honey, those are your hobbies. Now I need for you to think carefully about the question, there is no rush for the answer... Who are you?"

60

Realizing now that she does not need to rush to give me an answer, she thought for a bit, and the answer that came out next was eye opening, and it led me on a journey to not just understand myself, but to understand others.

My 10 year daughter replied, "well Dad, in a sort of proud way, I am a bit of a geek, and a nerd."

Intrigued by that response, I asked how she arrived at such an answer. She said, "I am a nerd because I wear glasses."

"Honey you wear glasses because your eyesight is not at 100%, but the glasses do not define who you are. How did you arrive at such an answer?"

"Well, Dad, my friends call me a nerd because I wear glasses."

Of course my reply at that time was, "First of all, those are not your friends if they tease you and give you labels, so be very careful of who you call your friend."

That interaction got me curious to ask the same question to some adult colleagues, and interestingly enough I discovered that many folks got their identity from how other people saw them, and not how they saw themselves. They chose careers, partnerships, what type of car they drove, even the foods or diets they consume, and everything else you can think of based on their adopted belief, never asking themselves where that identity came from and why they believed it to be true for them.

That question is the beginning to leading a

totally fulfilling life that you know you designed yourself, and not the way other people see you to be. As you have gathered by now, to truly be the Lady in the Streets, a woman must always have a clear knowledge of exactly who she is. As you discover your identity you will find that insecurities will disappear. As you observe people around you, and yes even some of your friends, you will notice that the ones with the most insecurities are the ones that may not have a clear knowledge of exactly who they are.

Chapter 7
The Freak in the Sheets

The Freak in the Sheets is not just about what happens behind closed doors. It is not even about sexual positions or acts in the bedroom, it is not about your shape, your size, your body type, the length of hair or the color of your skin. I have met and interviewed so many women that hold out from embracing their natural God-given sensuality and sexuality, because they tend to compare themselves to other women with different body types, and would say things like, "I would wear that type of outfit if or when I get to a size..."

Ladies — do not put off being the Freak in the Sheets for a certain look, because your man's patience may tend to expire, not to mention another self-confident woman who does not seem to care about what other people think of her will capture his attention. Learn to graciously accept his compliments that you are sexy and beautiful, and don't wait for the masses to confirm what he is saying to you. If you cannot see the beauty in yourself and keep putting intimacy on pause until you reach a certain goal, your man may be convinced to be attracted to that different body type and with someone who already is there.

The Freak in the Sheets is more of a way of thinking. Everything you have done in this life you have learned to do. That pretty head of yours has been the control tower that directed you to weed out, through reasoning, the wrong way to accomplish a goal. It has led you on to walk successfully for the first time, to talk, read, write, sing, swim, balance your checkbook, play blackjack... You get the picture? Your control tower is also going to be able to teach you to be a true Freak in the Sheets. All you have to do is relax, clear your head of those preconceived notions that have been stumbling blocks to sensuality, and open yourself up to new signals. Now Ladies, I do not care if you are built like a truck driver or a twig, there should be no excuses. You can attract any man worth your attention, drive him wild with pleasure and keep him coming back eagerly for more.

How exactly are you going to do this, you ask? There are four keys to unlocking your sensuality and becoming a true Freak in the Sheets.

1. Heightened Sensitivity

2. Appetite (Sexual)

3. The Desire to Give

4. Sexual Skills

I have found the reason many women have difficulty and struggles in this area is the fear of labels. Those labels are exactly the reason why your man may look elsewhere. My advice is to embrace

64

every label you can think of and instead of allowing the labels having a negative tone, put a positive spin on those labels. For instance, a common word used is "slut". How many positives spins you can put on that word? I have witnessed many men already in relationships chasing after the so called "slut". So, come up with a list of negative words or labels. The loose woman, Jezebel, hoe, bitch, skank, hooch, plus any number of other words or title you can come up with. It is fine if some of these labels you just cannot stand, and you can feel free to tell your partner which ones are off- limits. Now, put a positive spin on those words or labels if you can. I have found that the woman who embraces their titles seem to have the most fulfilling and exciting relationships, and their man never strays. Let us keep in mind this book is not about changing anyone; it is, however, about making changes in the way you **think**.

The Penis

Now, let us explore the male body — of course we will start with the penis. The penis is actually a pretty complex organ, and varies greatly from man to man in terms of shape, size, color, curvature, and sensitivity. This is very important to note, as many women may not know this, but over time each penis evolves, and its hot spots and responsiveness are redefined. This means that exploring his hot spots and gauging his reactions is not a one-shot deal. Even if you think you know a penis inside out, it is always good to get back to basics every couple of months to learn about its new sweet spots and sensitivities, and a true Freak in the Sheets can have lots of fun exploring and getting to know his most intimate and electrical parts.

The Anus

The butt hole is an area of many taboos for quite a few men, and if your man is not open to it, don't push the issue, simply talk and get to the true "why". Some men do, however, love to have their butt hole played with on the outside, others love to be penetrated, and of course others like to keep their anus a safe distance away from all foreign objects. Many men have made the statement that the anus is for exit only, and of course I say to each his own, but let us keep in mind that personal anal preference is entirely unrelated to sexual orientation. In that same region is the prostate; just like a woman's G-spot, the prostate is located inside the male body and can be accessed through the anus on its upper wall.

The Male Orgasm

The male sexual response is often played down in our culture; there is a mistaken assumption that all men are simple sexual beings... But this is not the case! Men are just as varied, complex, and unique as women are sexually, and they require both the physical and mental stimulation to enjoy that explosive sex.

Just like women, men tend to experience a range of physical responses to sexual stimulation with or without the desired mental responses, and that means getting your mind into the steamy hot game of sex is just as important for men. I am about to share with you some of the physical changes that men may experience during sexual response.

66

I would like for you to keep in mind that the male's body can act in mysterious ways, so these sensations and reactions can occur independently of each other and in a non-sequential fashion. News Flash!! For many men, sometimes penises decide to get rock hard for no good reason, and other times they decide they are not going to rise to the occasion, even though the rest of the body is ready to get down to some hot action. Ladies — don't take it personally if you may be putting on a super-hot performance and not getting quite the results you were hoping for, and always keep these very important facts in mind. A quick note to think about: an orgasm and ejaculation are two separate occurrences, because they normally happen simultaneously most women think that the ejaculation is the orgasm; the proof is in a man's erotic dreams, as a man can experience an orgasm in his dream and not always ejaculate.

Thoughts Turn To Sex, Intimacy, Romance, Eroticism, and Physical Connection

In this section I will give many examples submitted and suggested by many women around the world. It is up to you to choose some of the examples that best suit your personality and comfort level, keeping in mind that growth only happens after some sort of discomfort.

A true Freak in the Sheets always knows that a man's most responsive sexual organ is his head (no, not that head, the one with a brain). Let me explain. Men are very responsive to seeing sexy photos, pornography, phone sex, and any teasing messages of what you want to do to him. This will always get an immediate response from him. It has always been widely known that making love for a woman happens way before the bedroom. It was also thought that men are only about the physical. This cannot be further from the truth. It is just done differently, before the actual act. I can recall being so aroused before an actual encounter by suggestive thoughts mentioned by text or emails that are short and sweet, simply painting a picture of what I can expect. But I must say, you have to follow through on what you say you are going to do. There is nothing more disappointing than painting those pictures and then quickly erasing them because you were too tired or somehow ended up not being in the mood. Many women choose to refrain from getting into that type of teasing, but not doing anything at all can be worse. That will tend to start the beginning of resentment, and you certainly do not want that to occur.

Of course, if that man's most responsive sexual organ is his brain, that will suggest that strong communication skills will be a major benefit. A true Freak in the Sheets has a goal of keeping her man aroused all through the day without touching him, making him yearn just to be in her space. Many women who are like that say how much fun it is having their man eating out of the palm of their hands, and speaking as a man myself, there's nothing I won't do for my woman when she takes the time, the imagination, and creativity to go that extra mile just for me. I know many of you are thinking that this is a form of manipulation, but the reality is that when you are exercising the most sexual muscle in the human body, it can no way be manipulation.

Here is some info that you may or may not

already know: Many men, to prolong the sexual experience, will sometimes think about work or sports during lovemaking, to distract from having an orgasm, and women do the same thing as well — proof positive that the most responsive sexual organ is the brain for both sexes. Here are some examples presented to me by women I've interviewed:

Scenario 1

The two of you are out to dinner at a nice restaurant. You excuse yourself to go freshen up, you wait a few minutes and return to the table. While in the bathroom you slip off your sexy underwear (I hope you chose to wear sexy underwear) and as you return to the table you place the panties either in his hand or in his pocket. He will of course recognize or see what it is and at that point you will be lucky if he can make it through the end of dinner or make it all the way home before he is all over you.

Scenario 2

If you have a traveling-man, then this can be fun. Even though he may be thousands of miles away, a woman has the power to remind him of what is waiting for him when he gets home. With so much technology in our hands, women can and should use it to their advantage and maybe just for their man's eyes only. Send a sexy video of yourself, either doing something naughty or just dressed up in a sexy lingerie. This will get him aroused and will make him want to come home sooner than expected.

Scenario 3

You are at home and it is time for bed. Send him a text from inside the bathroom letting him know that you have something special planned. Put on your sexiest outfit, do your hair, put on your favorite lipstick (the one you know drives him crazy), put on your high heels and send him a couple more text messages before you emerge from the bathroom. He will be waiting with so much anticipation you may barely make it to the bed before he is all over you.

Scenario 4

Check your man's schedule, and when you find some free time book one night at a hotel or motel. For the sake of seducing his mind, the venue can also be a no frills motel. Arrange for him to meet you at the hotel, texting him the room number and ask him to notify you when he arrives in the parking lot. As you receive that notification, reply telling him to come right in, leaving the door propped open so that he can let himself in. As he enters he should find you ready and waiting for him. I promise you after a scenario like that he will be the one surprising you with similar outings.

Before I go on to the next very important point, I cannot stress enough the importance of open and honest communication about expectations, fantasies, and pleasures, since it is so important that the two of you are on the same page. This is a great opportunity for you to share your deepest desires, and if for any reason he feels intimidated, that will be a great opportunity to start a new conversation. Keep in mind that most negative responses and jealousy generally stem from some sort of fear. A good way to get him to talk about his fears is by simply sharing some of yours. I totally understand that to lay it all on the table is scary, especially since it makes you feel so vulnerable in front of your partner, but I ask you: isn't that what trust is all about?

Now let us take a moment and visit the oldest profession in the world; yes, I am talking about prostitution! I would also ask for this part of the chapter you refrain from judgments, which I'm sure you have done great at so far. I promise you that it will make lots of sense by the time I am done.

Have you ever realized that throughout time, some men have left their families, given up fortunes and careers, and like a drug keep going back for more and more? Some men even find themselves falling in love with these women, and some of these men are from all different walks of life — from blue collar to white collar, businessmen to celebrities, and even politicians. What is the secret? What strange power do these women have over some men? I am here to tell you there is no voodoo or tricks, simply seducing a man's largest and most responsive sexual organ: the brain.

A popular line used in many sex-work ads is "I will do everything your wife or girlfriend won't do."

A deeper look into that one liner is an opening for a man to share his deepest fantasy without the possibility of any judgments or labels, and the anticipation of performing that act he cannot seem to be open to discuss or do with his lady. Let's look at a couple of actual ads, and I challenge you to see if you can detect certain patterns in seducing a man's mind.

Ad 1:

> Hey baby! My name is * * * * * ! Tired
> of getting the same old thing at home?
> Had a long week? Whatever it is you
> are maybe going through, I'm here to
> help you escape into a fantasy land
> where YOU call the shots, and I will
> make your dreams come true! Get lost
> in my hazel eyes as we explore the
> curves that my soft body has to offer.
> My sweet, sexy, and sultry attitude
> will have you feeling at ease, relaxed,
> and comfortable.... As if you've known
> me forever! One visit will have you
> hooked and keep coming back for more.

Of course, this ad was accompanied with pictures of herself wearing lacy one-piece lingerie.

Ad 2:

Hi I'm * * * * * , a professional and
passionate luxury companion. I am
here to provide excellent pleasure,
and first-class companionship
services. As you and I both know,
many gentlemen enjoy spending their
precious downtime with beautiful and
sensually talented vixens like myself.
If you are looking for a woman to make
your travels exhilarating, your days
fulfilled, and your nights passionately
and erotically breathtaking, then
don't hesitate to book me.

I comprehensively understand the
best relationships come from a place
of loyalty and honesty, and I truly
care for and respect the feelings of the
men in my life. You are encouraged to
openly discuss what your requirements
and expectations are, as I will go
above and beyond to fulfill whatever
experience it is you desire. So, what
are you waiting for? Call or email to
book me now, and finally experience
how it feels to be treated like royalty.

Ad 3:

    Take a break from your exhausting
grind of the day and spoil yourself
with the new girl in town. I'm * * * * *
and I'm always ready for fun. Let me
give you that unforgettable experience
you need. My mission is to leave you

with a smile and treat you like a king.
Let yourself indulge in my soothing
company. Let us make a memory you
will never forget. I am only a call or
text away and I will come right over!

Take note that none of these ads mentioned anything sexual or explicit, and the pictures, while sexy with hair and makeup done, were never explicit in any way. Yet they most certainly align with what most men desire, and if they deliver on what the ad says, then they will have a man coming back for more and even falling head over heels for them. The man that spends the money to be with these women doesn't even care that these women's main motivation is the money, or even if there is sincerity in the ad. You must admit that it tends to grab a man's attention. I am in no way trying to glorify prostitution, and I'm in total acknowledgment of the epidemic of human trafficking that has become an unfortunate part of this profession. However, not all of these women are forced into that lifestyle. Many of them are independents, using the lifestyle as a true business, and are living a life of luxury and travels.

The key is to make your partner feel like whenever they are in your presence, they are all that matters. Allow them to explore fantasies, never stopping at just one, and discover new fantasies together, keeping in mind that fantasies explored between the both of you do not need to be always fulfilled. If for any reason you may think that your man does not deserve such a treatment, Then it may just be a matter of time that another woman will see the king in him and recognize the four men that he is.

Chapter 8

Summary

By now you have obviously seen several common themes from each chapter, so let's recap, shall we? First, know the true you, and stay true to yourself. Another person can see more clearly than you can give them credit for how you truly feel about yourself, and if you have low self-esteem the only type you will attract is the shark that senses weakness and sets out to take advantage of you. Now for a big one: open communication. Eliminate your fears of being judged and communicate how things truly are and not what you think your partner would want to hear, and if you sense that you are being judged by the other person, simply let them know. You can only achieve that level of communication if you are each other's best friend. Think about it this way: the moment we step out of our home, someone is passing some sort of judgment on us, from the clothes we wear, the car we drive, to the color of our skin. It is only fair to request that if you are in any type of relationship, your home should be a judgment- and label-free zone. I say label-free in the sense that, if your partner expresses a fantasy that may not fit into what you consider normal or see eye to eye with, refrain from labels like "you are sick" or "That is nasty". Labels will tend to cause your partner to close up, and in that closed place resentment begin to grow, and a need to reciprocate the wrong things.

Toward the completion of writing this book I had an amazing conversation with a couple I admire very much. They were one day after celebrating their thirty fourth wedding anniversary. After congratulating them I just had to ask them, "What is the secret to you two being married for thirty-four years and maintaining such a noticeable and obvious strong love?" The response was amazing and aligned very well with some of what we have spoken about in this book. The husband very calmly and confidently said that before they even went out on a first date, he laid everything on the table and was totally transparent about his love for drinking and other habits. He figured that if she was to accept him, it had to be for everything that he was at the time. Now while his potential girlfriend at the time, because she did not agree with his choice in lifestyle, determined to give him a chance and not rush to judgment, she told him, "I don't want to witness or see you doing any of those things around me". He agreed, and they went out on a first date. A strong love affair began.

Thirty-four years later the level of their open communication never wavered. Discussing the book with this couple and talking about the four men and the two women, without hesitation the wife said confidently that she indeed has all four of the men all the time. The husband confirmed at that moment that his wife is definitely the two women, and to demonstrate his full understanding of the

76

two women, he shared one of the conversations they had early in their relationship where his wife made it clear that she did not want for him to ever look anywhere further than herself, if he could think of anything he wanted to try or experiment with, bring it to her attention and they would discover it together.

As a couple, stay true to your roles all the time, know that in your relationship it is not a one-way street.

For the Men: Do not shoot the messenger! Many women have admitted that they cannot stand telling their man what they want, they somehow feel that if a man does something because he was asked to, then it is not from the heart or genuine, and that is a big deal for many women. Do not get too frustrated at this point, as the fact is that these women said that if their man were in all four roles, they would have no problem opening up more about their needs and their feelings. Many of them have even said that it would be easier to communicate with their partner! As the man, there is not an option to pick out of the four men, you must be all four. Your lady will confirm this anytime you ask, but do however feel free to be an over achiever in these four roles, as your confidence level will be even more heightened than ever before and it will pay off ten-fold. As part of being honest with yourself, by now you can definitely identify which one or more of the four men you are not. However, put in the work to embrace the lacking roles, and I am confident you can be that new man, and begin the journey to your partner falling in love with you all over again. Trust me! There is another level beyond what you may be experiencing in your present relationship.

For the Ladies: Embrace your roles, it's only fair that if your man put in the work to be those four men, he should be with his two women, and you can trust that when he embraces the roles, other women will begin to notice. There were so many women that when I gave certain examples of the four men, their first response was, "where can I find a man like that?"

Ladies — your peers are paying close attention, some were open enough to mention how lucky my wife must be. Also, these roles should not be something that is turned on and off, these roles should not be used as some sort of bargaining chip, or a reward for good behavior. It is an awareness to be a part of who you are, without changing who you are. Attraction to another person is very unique to each one of us, so discover your very own signature in each one of the roles, and have lots of fun doing it!

About the Author

Born in the Caribbean Islands of Trinidad and Tobago, I have been blessed to be a product of a very loving environment. I had a very hard-working dad who never lost sight of making certain his family was never in need, and a Mom whose faith runs deep, and always kept the household grounded. I have one brother and one sister, both older. Yes, I am the baby of the family! My sister was also instrumental in helping to raise her baby brother as my Mom decided to begin a career in banking. The success of their two careers enabled the family to experience the world at a very young age. Thanks to that environment, it was from an early age that I understood what unconditional love really meant, and to this day the support structure remains unwavering, and only gets stronger.

Let us jump ahead to my pre-teen years. My parents were invited to an evening gala at a very prestigious corporate attorney's home, and there was no one to babysit me since both my brother and sister had made plans. The host of the event told my parents that they could bring me along, and that the house was large with different items to keep me entertained. Upon arriving, I was led to a den area, where there was a TV, a VCR with a collection of movies, and a record player with a collection of records. "Wow! You mean I could play some music?" I asked with a gleam in my eyes. I was at that time extremely fascinated with putting the needle to a record, and knew all the popular songs that I listened to on the radio, and now it was my turn to do like the DJs on the radio did.

My parents — who ran a tight ship, and always wanted us to be on our best behavior whenever we were out — said, "NO WE DON'T WANT YOU PLAYING WITH THE RECORD PLAYER, YOU MAY BREAK IT!"

The Host then said, "It's okay, he can play all the music that he wants! We will be on the other side of the house and the music will not disturb us at all."

I was in heaven! I can play music for hours and not get tired, and that's what I started doing. The collection of music was great! After about two hours of playing music, around 11:00pm, the Host comes into the room to check in on me. "I AM DOING GREAT!" I shouted with a big grin on my face. He left to join his guests, however he left the door open. Not wanting to disturb the adults with my loud music, I got up and closed the door. Shortly after he returned again, and once again left the door open. However, this time as I went over to close it again, he stopped me. "No need to close the door, we're all enjoying the music!"

I look around him, and to my amazement, the gathering had migrated over to an open area outside the den, and some of the male guests had even moved some furniture around so they could dance. By this time it is now about 2:00am, and things are now coming to a close. As the guests are leaving they are commenting to the host. "What a great time! And such a great idea hiring a DJ! Make sure you have the same DJ next year!"

At 10 years old I discovered the happiness that I can bring to people through music. I loved the feeling. That was the beginning of my journey to becoming a professional DJ. However at 10 saying that you want to become a DJ does not necessarily promise a bright future.

Now in my teen years, I began noticing girls more, and also have a curiosity on how electronics like record players and televisions actually work. Little did I realize that same curiosity is what would lead me to writing a book like this. Being a bit sheltered, I knew as I entered my adulthood at 18, that I was a bit naive, and while I had had girlfriends, relationships did not seem to last, and I would sometimes lose a girlfriend or two to another guy. Approaching and talking to a girl was never difficult for me, so I never felt like there was something wrong with me whenever a girlfriend decided she wanted to be with someone else. However this one day, I'm outside my job (as an electronic technician) and I notice this beautiful girl walking down the sidewalk. She had such an exotic look about her (as most women in Trinidad do, the melting pot of African, East Indian, Spanish, French to name a few, produces a unique look and appearance that cannot fit into any stereotypical box). I approached this beautiful young lady and started a conversation, I asked her out to a new nightclub with my friends and some of her friends so there would be no uncomfortable feelings, and she agreed! I was so excited to get to know this young lady, and I recruited my good friend to drive us to the club, since I did not yet have a car. As we arrived to pick her up, she informed us that her friends backed out of going along, however she felt comfortable enough to go with us. On the ride to the club I noticed that she was quite chatty with my buddy, but I did not think much about it since this was supposed to be a first date.

As we arrived at the club I ordered a first round of drinks, and asked my lady-interest if she would like to dance. She replied "I don't really like that song being played maybe later". However, she was exhibiting quite a bit of interest in my friend, and kept turning down my requests to dance. A certain song came on that she really seemed to like, and I thought to myself that this was the chance I was waiting for! Instead, she turned to my friend and asked him to dance! I did not need any clearer sign that she was not interested in me and had developed a flame for my good friend. To think it all happened within a short time! I was impressed, as I had never seen my friend in action like that before, however he felt quite uneasy and started turning down her request to dance.

Shortly after our young lady was requesting for us to take her home, and after we dropped her off, on the ride home my good friend apologized profusely for the very odd scenario, to which I replied "Not a problem at all, I had just met her anyway." My friend owned a gym, and I was a trainer there, most of the clientele were women, and I taught one of the aerobics classes, but I must

82

say these women all had other motives. After class a few would stay back and just hang around my friend, as there was something about him that was like a magnet to these ladies.

A couple days later before one of our classes began, the phone rang and it was for my buddy. It was our young lady from a couple nights ago, and she had sought him out by the gym name and wanted to ask him out. In my presence he told her that there was no way would he go out with her, and unless she wants to join the gym there was no reason for her to call back. After he hung up, he once again apologized to me. "Wow! What is this draw you have with women? They all just want to get a piece of you" He said nothing, but reached into a drawer, and took out a book and hands it to me, The Sensuous Man. "Just read this and tell me what you think". I read the book, and that started my journey to becoming a true Sensuous Man. I must say it really worked.

The book is no longer in print and is really dated with some of its content. Along with my discovery of wanting to make people happy through music, I also wanted to be the best Sensuous Man I could be to any woman that I would be in a relationship with, and ultimately my wife one day. I would discover later on in life that achieving a lasting and fulfilling relationship required more than just being a Sensuous Man. I purchased my very own copy after I completed reading it. I would definitely share this secret with any of my male friends that would be willing to listen, however because of male egos and pride, many would turn a deaf ear to my new discovery.

The Sensuous Man opened my eyes to various sensual and sexual exercises, and so many erogenous zones in a woman's body I just had to learn more, so I purchased The Sensuous Woman. I wanted to learn sensuality from the women's perspective, and did it ever pay off!

The next level was my fascination about the female body, the latest discovery at that time was a woman's G-Spot. While other men at that time were being selfish lovers, I was experiencing great pleasures from the various types of orgasms I can produce in a woman's body. To this day I still believe that was the main reason I did not become a parent at such an early age as my peers, as I discovered greater pleasures without the need for actual penetration. Next was my exploration into the world of Kama Sutra, another book called The One Hour Orgasm, and my thirst for knowledge kept on needing to be quenched. To this day I still get the odd stares as I pick-up a Cosmopolitan Magazine, but to all the guys out there who really want to be desirable to his lady, there's a wealth of information in just that one magazine. What is interesting is that information is only being shared among women, and not reaching the men who can really benefit from it. And since each one of us are being judged in some sort of way, embrace the judgment. So what if people think you are gay! As long as you have a satisfied, fulfilled woman in your bed, the two of you will know you are not.

Printed in Great Britain
by Amazon

42944414R00050